SWIMMERS!

Curious Kids Press

Beavers

The beaver is in the rodent family. In fact, it is the second largest (the largest is the capybara). This animal is best known for building dams. The North American beaver's numbers once reached around 60 million, but now has been reduced to about 6 million. This is due to extensive hunting of this animal for its pelt. The beaver is an industrious animal and really cool. Let's explore the world of this rodent to see what else we can discover. Read on..

Where in the World?

Did you know there are beavers in Europe? The Eurasian beaver is found in Europe. The North American beaver can be found in Canada, throughout the United States and into parts of northern Mexico. It will always live by a water source, like rivers or wetlands, where it can build its dam and be safe from predators.

The Body of a Beaver

Did you know the beaver has a stocky body? Beavers continue to grow throughout their lifetime. Males can reach weights of around 55 pounds. Females will be smaller. Their legs are shorter with webbed back feet. Their front paws have 5 toes on each paw. Each toe has a sharp claw on the end of it.

The Beaver's Tail

Did you know the tail of a beaver is really flat? This rodent has a large flat tail that is shaped like a paddle for a boat. The beaver's tail helps steer this animal when it is moving logs to its dam. Its tail is also black and scaley. When the beaver is on land, its broad tail helps it balance when it is carrying heavy loads.

The Beaver's Fur

Did you know the beaver's fur is very thick? It has 2 layers; long fur on top and short fine hairs underneath. The top coat keeps this animal waterproof, while the undercoat keeps the beaver warm. The beaver needs to groom to keep its coat waterproof. An oily substance called, castor, is produced by the beaver. It spreads the castor around its body by grooming.

The Beaver's Teeth

Did you know the beaver has 2 huge front teeth? This animal's front teeth stick out the front of its mouth. This is so the beaver can cut wood while underwater. The beaver's teeth are very sharp and can saw through small trees and branches. This animal's teeth never stop growing, so chewing on tough trees, helps keep them trim.

What a Beaver Eats

Did you know the beaver only eats the bark from wood, not the entire branch? Beavers only eat plants. This makes them, vegetarians. This animal likes to eat cattail shoots in the spring and summer months. In the autumn and winter seasons, the beaver will eat shrubs and tree bark.

The Beaver's Dam

Did you know the beaver's dam can be harmful to humans? A beaver's dam will change the natural flow of a river or a lake. This can sometimes create flooding for the area it is in. The beaver works all night to build a basic dam. It uses mud, stones and sticks it has collected.

The Beaver's Lodge

Did you know the beaver makes a home called, a lodge? Lodges can either be surrounded by water or on the banks of a shore. The lodge is made from sticks and mud. There are at least 2 water-filled tunnels leading in and out of the lodge. Beavers do not hibernate and will store sticks for food.

Inside the Beaver Lodge

Did you know the beaver's lodge is warm and dry inside? The beaver's home has a big chamber for eating, sleeping and to groom and raise their young. This mammal will collect soft materials like, grasses, reeds and wood chips for its bedding. It is changed often to keep its home neat and tidy.

The Beaver as Prey

Did you know the beaver has many predators? This rodent is hunted by a lot of predators, both big and small. Common predators of the beaver include the lynx, owls, wolverines, bears, coyotes, northern river otters, wolves and hawks. People also still hunt the beaver for its pelt and occasionally its meat.

Beaver Talk

Did you know the beaver uses its tail to make a loud "slapping" sound on the water? This is done when the beaver is alarmed. A beaver can hiss and snort when it is upset.or whine when it is in pain. Another sound is "churring." This is a sign of contentment. Soft mumbling noises may mean the beaver has a lot on his mind.

The Beaver Mom and Dad

Did you know beavers pair for life? Adult beavers will find one mate and stay with that one until one of them dies. Both the male and female beavers build the lodge. After mom has her babies, she will care for them, while dad defends the lodge and his family.

Baby Beavers

Did you know baby beavers are called, kits?
Baby beavers are born in a litter of up to 6 kits.
They are born in the lodge where they will nurse
milk from their mother. Kits will remain with the
parents until they are about 2 years-old. At this
time they will leave to start their own family.

Life of a Beaver

Did you know beavers are very social? Beavers live in family units consisting of a mother, father, 2 year-old kits and newborn young. Sometimes beavers will build an addition onto their lodge when the family gets too big. If left alone to thrive, beavers can live to be around 24 years old.

Polar Bears

There is only one species of the polar bear. In science, it is called, Ursus maritimus. This means "sea bear." The polar bear is the largest land predator and also the largest of all the bear species. The Inuit peoples have great respect for this bear. It is called, Nanuk. When they write about this animal they call it, Pihoqahiak. This means, the ever-wandering one. These fun facts are just the tip of the iceberg when it comes to the polar bear. Read on to discover more.

Where in the World?

Did you know the polar bear loves the ice and snow? This big burly bear lives mostly in the Arctic Circle, in the Arctic Ocean and all its areas. The polar bear loves the ice and the frigid waters of the Arctic and will spend a lot of its time in the water.

The Body of a Polar Bear

Did you know polar bears are huge? Male polar bears can weigh up to 1,700 pounds! Females are smaller at about 600 pounds, but still very big. Adult males of this species can reach lengths of 10 feet long - that is as tall as a 1 story building!

Polar Bear Paws

Did you know the paws on this bear are suited to both water and snow? The polar bear's paws are huge - 12 inches across! On the bottom of the polar bear's big feet are pads covered with little bumps. These keep the bear from slipping on the ice and snow.

The Polar Bear's Fur

Did you know this bear's fur is waterproof? The polar bear's fur has 2 layers to it; a thick, short undercoat and longer top hairs. Even though the polar bear may appear to be white in color, the hairs on its coat are actually transparent (see through). Under the fur, this bear's skin is black to absorb the sunlight.

What a Polar Bear Eats

Did you know polar bears only eat meat? This type of animal is called, a carnivore. The main diet of the polar bear consists of the seal species. This bear has 42 teeth. They are very sharp and perfect for eating meat. The canine teeth (near the front) are longer and are used for grabbing and holding its prey.

The Polar Bear as a Predator

Did you know this bear is a still-hunter? The polar bear uses its excellent sense of smell to locate a seal. This is usually outside of a small hole in the ice the seal uses for getting air. When the seal comes up for a breath, the polar bear reaches in with its massive paw and drags it out.

The Polar Bear as Prey

Did you know the polar bear has no natural enemies, except man? The native people of the Arctic region hunted the polar bear for its hide and its meat. Every part of the bear was used. However, the native people only hunted the bear when it was needed. The polar bear is now protected from being poached.

The Polar Bear's Special

Did you know even though the polar bear is big, it is fast? This bear is an excellent swimmer. It spends a lot of time in the water. The polar bear can reach speeds of up to 6.2 miles-per-hour. The polar bear can also swim long distances - up to 62 miles without stopping.

Polar Bear Talk

Did you know this species of bear makes sounds? Adult polar bears mostly make sounds when they are unhappy. An angry polar bear may growl, hiss, chuff or champ its teeth together. Baby polar bears will whimper, squall, hiss and smack their lips. Mom polar bear will warn her cubs by chuffing or braying.

Polar Bear Mom

Did you know a female polar bear can have her young at 4 to 5 years of age? She will only breed about every 3 years. Mom polar bear will gain a lot of weight - over 400 extra pounds! She will build a den in the snow to have her young in.

Polar Bear Baby

Did you know baby polar bears are called, cubs? The cubs are born with soft fuzzy fur, they are blind and helpless. Usually, the female will have only 2 cubs, weighing around 2 pounds each. They nurse milk from their mother. Cubs will remain with mom for around 2.5 years.

Polar Bears at Rest

Did you know the polar bear likes to sleep on the ice and snow? This bear can rest in many positions. Sometimes it is sprawled out with all four legs spread. Other times, this bear may tuck its front legs under its chest. Often times it will sleep on its side.

Polar Bears at Play

Did you know this species of bear likes to play? A polar bear will engage in play fighting. This can be done by cubs, or by two young males learning how to fight. Although, the polar bear is mostly a solitary animal, it has been seen embracing and playing with other bears for hours on end.

Life of a Polar Bear

Did you know the polar bear usually lives to be 25 years-old? In the wild most polar bears rarely live past 25; however, one polar bear did live until she was 43 years-old. This bear was in captivity. Old or injured polar bears will usually die of starvation because they can no longer hunt for food.

Sea Otters

Sea otters are related to weasels. They are in the Mustelidae family and the biggest animal in this category. Other animals in this family include the badgers, wolverines and polecats. This animal is a favorite at many zoos and marine parks because of its playful and whimsical nature. It is thought the otter has been around for about 5 million years. If you think these facts are cool, you "otter" read on to discover more about this interesting animal.

Where in the World?

Did you know sea otters live most of their lives in the water? They can be found in the northern and eastern North Pacific Ocean. These animals live off shore and in kelp beds. They can also be found where there are plenty of places to dive down and to forage for food on the seafloor.

The Body of a Sea Otter

Did you know the body of a sea otter is built for swimming? The sea otter is a heavy animal. Males can weigh up to 99 pounds and females about 73 pounds. It has webbed feet on its back legs and a long tail. Its legs are shorter and its body is long and sleek.

The Sea Otter Fur

Did you know the fur on a sea otter is extremely thick? It has 1 million hairs in 1 square inch of fur! This makes the fur the densest of any other mammal. Its fur has 2 layers; long waterproof guard hairs (hair on top) and a thick short undercoat. This keeps the otter from becoming cold in the water.

What a Sea Otter Eats

Did you know the sea otter hunts for food in the water? This mammal will eat snails, clams, mussels, fish and small organisms found on sea kelp. It forages for food along the ocean floor. It can hold its breath up to 5 minutes. However, most of its dives only last about a minute.

The Sea Otter's Special

Did you know this mammal uses rocks as tools? The sea otter will use its favorite sharp rock to crack open the shells of its prey. It can also move rocks and dig through the mud on the bottom of the sea floor. This is where it finds and picks up clams to eat.

The Sea Otter's "Pouch"

Did you know this animal has a "pouch?" The sea otter has an extra flap of skin under each of its front legs. This acts like a pouch to hold and carry things in. The otter will store its favorite rock, clams and other food that it has foraged, in this extra skin. Once it surfaces, the otter will use its rock to split open and eat its find.

Sea Otters at Rest and

Did you know the sea otter likes to slide? When in zoos or marine exhibits you may notice the otters running and sliding. This is a form of play. In the wild, otters will sleep and rest in a group. This is called, a raft. Sea otters in large groups may hold each other's front paws while floating on their backs.

The Sea Otter as Prey

Did you know sea otters were hunted by man? This species almost became extinct because of overhunting. The sea otter's fur was used to make clothes from. Predators in the wild like sharks, orcas and eagles will also hunt the sea otter, especially the very young, old or injured sea otters.

Sea Otter Talk

Did you know the sea otter can make sounds? A sea otter can scream and whistle. This animal will grunt and coo when it is enjoying a meal. During the mating season, male otters will coo or make a whining, dog-like sound. An angry or frightened otter will sometimes hiss or even snarl.

Mom Sea Otter

Did you know a female sea otter can have young at 3 to 4 years-old? Once pregnant, she will carry her young for around 3 to 4 months. The mother sea otter will give birth to 1 baby otter in the water. Some types of otters will have 2 babies per year.

Baby Sea Otters

Did you know baby sea otter is called, a pup?
The pup looks like a fuzzy little ball when it is
born. The hair on it is very dense and helps it
float. The pup will ride around on its mother's
chest and belly when she is floating. It nurses
milk from her, which is very high in fat.

Life of a Sea Otter

Did you know sea otters can live to be 15 years-old? Sea otters spend their time foraging for food and floating on their backs. These animals are very smart and social. In addition, they keep the kelp forests healthy. They do this by eating the sea urchin that feed on the kelp.

The Northern Sea Otter

This sea otter can grow up to 5 feet in length and weigh around 100 pounds. Females of this breed are smaller. It can be brown, black or even silver in color. Its front paws have strong toes and the back ones are webbed for swimming. They have small ears and cute faces.

The Giant Sea Otter

This otter is closely related to the sea otter. It is the largest member of this family. It can measure up to 5.6 feet long. It has a sleek body and is active all day long. It eats mostly fish and crabs. It has the shortest hair of all the breeds. It is usually chocolate brown in color.

Walrus

The walrus is a large mammal that belongs to the, Odobenidae family. Its name in Latin means, "tooth-walking sea-horse." The walrus has been around for a long time. In fact, a walrus fossil was found in the San Francisco Bay. It is estimated to be about 28,000 years old. The walrus has lots of other interesting and fascinating facts to go along with it, as well. Let's explore the world of the walrus to discover more about this weird mammal.

Where in the World?

Did you know the walrus loves cold climates? This animal can be found around the North Pole, the Arctic ocean and both the North Atlantic and North Pacific oceans. It lives most of its life in the shallow waters and on ice flows. During the breeding season it will come ashore and lounge around in a large group.

The Body of a Walrus

Did you know the walrus has a very small head? The body of a walrus is roundish and is built more for moving in the water than on land. It has 2 large flippers on its front and 2 smaller flippers on its hind end. The walrus's ears are inside its tiny head. It has small wide-set eyes.

The Size of the Walrus

Did you know the walrus is bulky and huge? Some walrus can exceed weights of 4,000 pounds! The skin of the walrus is very thick - up to 6 inches. This tough skin and a thick layer of fat called, blubber, helps keep this animal warm in the frosty weather.

Walrus Tusks

Did you know the tusks of a walrus are made from ivory? Both the male and female walrus have tusks. These continue to grow throughout the walrus's lifetime. The male's tusks will be longer and wider. These tusks are considered very valuable. Man has poached this animal for the ivory in its tusks.

The Job the Tusks

Did you know the walrus uses its tusks to do many things? The tusks of the walrus help to pull this animal along on shore. The tusks are used to dig through the bottom of the ocean to find food and to also crack open the shells. Males use their long sharp tusks to show dominance and to attract a mate.

What a Walrus Eats

Did you know the walrus may only eat every few days? The walrus hunts for clams, mussels, cockles and other shellfish that live on the bottom of the ocean. The walrus can dive down 300 feet in search of food. One walrus can eat around 4,000 clams in one day.

Walrus Whiskers

Did you know the whiskers on a walrus are very sensitive? The whiskers on a walrus are called, vibrissae. These 6 inch whiskers cover the walrus's entire snout. When hunting for food under water, the vibrissae of the walrus can feel where the food is. These whiskers are constantly being worn down.

The Social Walrus

Did you know the walrus is very social? This big animal loves to be with other walruses. They will group together on large ice floes or on land. A herd of walrus can contain as many as 1,000 individuals. They will even pile on top of each other. This group is made up of males, females and their young.

The Walrus as Prey

Did you know the walrus only has 3 predators? Polar bears hunt the walrus on land and will take the young and weaker members of a herd. Orca (Killer Whales) hunt the walrus in the ocean. The third predator is man. Humans hunt this animal for its meat, blubber and tusks.

Walrus Talk

Did you know the walrus can make sounds? The walrus can make a range of noises from grunts, whistles, growls and bellows - it kind of sounds like Chewbacca from Star Wars. Most of the sound the walrus makes is done in the breeding season to attract a mate or when it feels threatened.

The Walrus Mom

Did you know the female walrus may not have a baby until she is 10 years-old? The walrus reproduce very slowly. Mom walrus (or cow) will carry her calf for 15 to 16 months. She will give birth to just one calf between the months of April and June. She nurses the baby walrus in the water.

The Baby Walrus

Did you know the baby walrus is born huge? A walrus calf can weigh as much as 165 pounds when it is first born! The calf is born already knowing how to swim. In the herd, a mother walrus will keep her calf safe under her two front flippers. The calf will stay with its mother for about 2 years.

Life of a Walrus

Did you know the walrus can live a very long time? A healthy walrus can live to be 40 years old. Some walrus have been put into special exhibits and zoos. These walrus can be trained and are very entertaining. Mostly the walrus will spend its life, eating sleeping and swimming.

Pacific Walrus

Although there is only species of walrus, the Pacific walrus is the biggest of the subspecies. This giant can exceed weights of 4,000 pounds. It spends over half of its life in the cold waters of the Arctic. There are about 200,000 of the Pacific walrus in the world today.

Thank you for checking out another addition from Curious Kids Press! Make sure to check out Amazon.com for many other great titles.

www.ingramcontent.com/pod-product-compliance
Lightning Source LLC
Chambersburg PA
CBHW040324010626
45792CB00024B/2114